My Best Kept Secret *Memoir*

My Best Kept Secret *Memoir*

Written by

Chioma Chime

Encounter with a Kind and Trustworthy Neighbor

When I was a child, my father had a job that required him to frequently travel from state to state or city to city. At first, I enjoyed the constant movement, but soon it began to negatively impact mine and my siblings' education. To address this issue, my parents made the decision for my mother and older siblings to settle in one city, while my immediate older sister and I would accompany our father wherever his work took him. This choice was based on the fact that moving had a greater impact on their schooling, as they needed consistency, while my sister and I were still in the early stages of education, attending kindergarten and early elementary school.

I was thrilled to be able to go with my father because it meant we would be constantly traveling and experiencing new places. We moved to a new city and state where we didn't know anyone, except for a family friend who lived about forty minutes away from us. In this unfamiliar city, if you encountered someone who spoke your language, they instantly became a part of your extended family, regardless of any blood relation.

We had a neighbor who was a single male

and happened to be from a state close to ours. He spoke our language, so he instantly became like an uncle to us. He portrayed himself as a responsible and respectable man, hailing from a humble and honorable family. He dedicated his time to his work and preferred to keep to himself. Specifically, he worked as an electrician for a local electric company. But enough about our neighbor for now.

A few days after we moved into our new home, we were enrolled in a school within the district. We had to start attending school right away because our father needed to get back to work. Meanwhile, our parents had hired a nanny to travel with us, but unfortunately, she couldn't make it on time. She assured us that she would join us within the week. The nanny had requested my father to enroll her in a computer program, so she could have a backup skill once we no longer required her services.

When the nanny failed to show up within the promised timeframe, my father began to feel frustrated because he needed to return to work. That's when our honorable, respectful, and responsible neighbor came to our rescue. He kindly volunteered to watch over us after school and help us with our schoolwork until our nanny could finally join us. My innocent father was overjoyed and relieved to have such a trusted and kind neighbor in our midst.

Before this incident, our neighbor had invited us to his apartment and was thoroughly impressed with our behavior. He spoke highly of us to our father, praising our good manners and behavior. I believe this played a part in his decision to offer to take care of us after school.

Prior to our neighbor's kind offer, our father had given us a lecture on how important it was to behave well and not annoy our neighbor. By the way, I forgot to mention our ages earlier. I had just turned six, while my sister had recently celebrated her eighth birthday. Being away from home and familiar faces, we always looked out for each other. Despite being normal siblings with occasional disagreements and fights, we were fiercely protective of one another. If you ever dared to come between us during a disagreement, we would instantly join forces and fight against you. I have always loved my sister dearly, and her happiness has consistently been my top priority. I would go to great lengths to protect her, as if I were the older sibling.

Our kind neighbor began taking care of us after school and even assisted us with our schoolwork. He had a remarkable talent for mathematics and wanted us to excel in that subject, aiming for us to be ahead of our peers. The initial weeks went smoothly, and we all started to grow accustomed to each other's presence. Witnessing his exceptional care, my father offered to pay him since he was essentially fulfilling the role of the absent nanny, who had yet to arrive due to personal matters before relocating to a different state. However, our neighbor declined the payment, stating that it was his pleasure to help.

On some days, we would visit our family friend who lived around thirty-five to forty minutes away from us. They had a house helper who was around the same age as my older sister or perhaps a year older, along with a baby. We loved going there to play with the baby, as they were essentially the only family we had in the area. Since our father was okay with us visiting, we began going there more frequently, especially since it was within walking distance if we took the shortcuts. However, our pseudo-nanny did not appreciate this arrangement, as he had grown accustomed to spending time with us. To handle the situation, he devised a technique where you would be rewarded (such as being allowed to visit our family friend's house or play outside with other neighborhood children) if you completed tasks as he asked, but you would face punishment if you failed to do things correctly.

On certain days, our neighbor would give us a multiplication table and assign each of us a specific table to learn. We were expected to memorize the entire table and present it to him when we were ready. Missing even a single number was not an option. To avoid his scrutiny, I would try to cram the table, but he was clever and would randomly ask multiplication questions to test whether we had truly learned or merely memorized. I always fell for it, and my punishment would be to stay behind while my sister got to go out and play or visit our family friend's house.

There were also times when he would ask us to help trim his toenails. It's quite amusing because, at such a young age, I couldn't even trim my own nails properly. If I didn't trim his nails the right way, I would, of course, face punishment.

Our neighbor had a strict rule against taking naps after school, and we were well aware of it. However, one day, thinking we were clever, we returned home from school to find him absent. Seizing the opportunity, we decided to lock our door and take a nap. While we were peacefully sleeping, I suddenly sensed someone's presence in our house. I squeezed my eyes shut tightly, refusing to look. The person entered our bedroom and waited for us to wake up. When we didn't, he left and went to his own apartment, where he double-twisted two wires. As an electrician working for an electric company, he had loose wires in his apartment. Upon returning to our room, he hit the wire on the bed, presumably to wake us up. However, we had already made up our minds to continue napping. We pretended to be asleep until the twisted wires landed on our backs. In pain and shock, we jumped off the bed, crying. He then informed us that our punishment for napping instead of studying was that we would not be allowed to go to our family friend's house for a week.

After three or four days, he lifted the ban but with a condition. Whoever completed their tasks correctly would be permitted to go outside and play with other children or visit our family friend's house.

It was during that month when everything took a dark turn. As I mentioned before, our neighbor had a habit of allowing my sister to go out and play while making me stay behind to learn my lessons, as I had not completed my tasks correctly. However, something sinister started happening. Sometimes, my sister would intentionally do her tasks incorrectly, hoping to receive the same punishment as me. But instead of being treated equally, she would be whipped with the twisted wires. We were unable to convince our father that the neighbor was abusing us, primarily because we were excelling in school, thanks to the "nice" neighbor. Additionally, our neighbor would present a different story to our father, showcasing himself as a caring and responsible man who would never harm anyone, not even a fly. He seemed to live a double life, behaving differently depending on the situation. When others were present, he would appear kind and responsible, but when alone with us, his true, monstrous personality emerged. He became a terrifying figure who would harm any small creature around him.

No one believed us when we tried to express our grievances about his mistreatment and abuse. The physical abuse went unnoticed, let alone the unspeakable sexual abuse.

It all began with consoling hugs whenever

my sister and I were separated, as we would both cry - she outside and I inside. Over time, these hugs turned into carrying us on laps and cuddling, eventually becoming a habit. During the first week of caring for us, there were no conditions, ultimatums, or punishments; it was a positive experience. However, as the second week progressed, he gradually began implementing punishments. Towards the end of that week, the hugs started again, but this time it was because I would become emotional when I made mistakes in my work. He would hold me close to his chest and tell me that he was going to teach me a trick, making me promise not to share it with my sister, as I was becoming his favorite. This "secret trick" involved him pulling my underwear off and inserting one of his fingers into me. I pulled away and started crying, but he convinced me that it was nothing harmful, just a confusing trick. When he asked if it was hurting me, I looked at him with tear-filled eyes and nodded my head "yes". Despite my distress, he didn't stop, but reassured me that it would be less painful next time, as that was how the trick was supposed to go. He allowed me to go out and play with the other children in the neighborhood, but made me promise again not to tell anyone, threatening harm to my entire family if I did.

After a few days of these inappropriate acts, he decided it was time for his sexual abuse to escalate. On a fateful day, he tested our knowledge by asking us questions about our schoolwork, and because we answered correctly, he decided that we should trim his toenails. I was terrible at it, as usual, and my sister was sent to our aunt's house while I was left inside. I couldn't contain my emotions and burst into tears, which led my sister to cry and beg him to forgive me, emphasizing that I was just a child. She offered to trim my assigned toenails herself, but he threatened that our behavior would result in us not being allowed to go to our aunt's house for a week. Holding onto me, she whispered a promise to tell our aunt about how the trusted neighbor had been treating us. We were then separated, with my sister running out and me being pulled back inside. He kept blaming me for his actions towards my sister and me, claiming that it was because I couldn't do anything right. He made me sit in a corner until I cried myself to sleep. When he heard me crying, he approached me and took me to his bedroom, laying me on his bed. In my innocence, I thought he was being kind, allowing me to sleep in his bed since the floor was uncomfortable. With my bloodshot eyes tightly closed, I heard him unbuckling his belt. I curled up in bed, expecting him to use his belt on me as he had done before. However, when I didn't feel any whipping, I started to relax, thinking he was simply changing his pants. After a few moments of silence,

I felt his hand on my shoulder, turning me onto my back. Confused, I gazed at him with innocent eyes, but my gaze seemed to trigger something in him, causing him to yell at me and demand that I shut my eyes. I quickly complied. He warned me that if I ever mentioned what he was about to show me to anyone, he would lock my sister in his room and whip her until her back and buttocks were soaked in her own blood. Realizing that whatever he was about to do wouldn't be good and that it would hurt, I started crying. He asked if I understood his threats, and although I nodded my head, I promised myself that I would endure anything to protect my sister from such brutality. Trying to distract myself, I suddenly felt something similar to an elbow pushing into me. I let out a scream that could have alerted the entire neighborhood, but he covered my mouth with one hand while forcing himself upon me. I was only six years old. I lay there, crying, and I believe I passed out from the pain, only to come back to consciousness later. When he was finished and satisfied with himself, he cleaned me up with wet cloths because there was blood all over my thighs and his sheet. I was still crying when my sister returned home and noticed the blood on me. She asked if he had whipped me again after she left, but I couldn't answer her question; I just continued crying.

Our father's job sometimes required him to be out of the city for a few days, which is why he needed a live-in nanny for us. On that particular day, I prayed that our father wouldn't come home because I didn't want him to find out about what had happened to me. It would have gotten my sister and me into severe trouble. Fortunately, our father didn't come home that day or the next. When I woke up the following day, I couldn't move my legs and my pelvic area and thigh were swollen. I also had a high temperature and my eyes were swollen from crying. I couldn't go outside. My confused sister kept asking what was wrong with me, and she turned to the nice neighbor for help. Luckily, it was the weekend and our first weekend without our father. The neighbor came to me and asked what was wrong. Seeing him brought tears to my eyes because I knew he would continue to hurt me, and I felt helpless. Unfortunately, I was right. He didn't stop at one or two times; it happened multiple times. He demanded that I get out of bed and clean myself up. I managed to get into the shower, and since he knew what was happening, he didn't want my sister to help me. He asked my sister to get some pain relievers and fever reducers for me and told me to make sure I had enough warm water around the swollen areas. When our father finally came home the next day, he noticed that something was wrong with me. The kind neighbor told him that I had gotten sick the previous day and was still recovering.

You might be wondering why our aunt didn't say anything to our father. Funny enough, sometimes when my sister would go to her house without me, the neighbor would ask my sister to tell our aunt that I refused to do my schoolwork, and he kept me back to finish it. Other times, he would tell my sister to lie and say that I was tired and decided to take a nap. Our aunt had her own issues to worry about and didn't pay much attention to what was happening with us.

Our father noticed that I was walking with a slight limp, but I convinced him that we were playing and I fell, hurting my leg, and that I would be fine. Fortunately for me, after more than a month of torture at the hands of the neighbor, the long-awaited nanny finally arrived. As soon as she arrived, the abuse drastically reduced. The whippings and sexual abuse stopped because she was always with us. We felt relieved because the neighbor shifted his attention to the young, beautiful, single nanny. However, this didn't last long. The nanny had family in a city about an hour and thirty minutes away, and she requested some days off to visit them. Our father agreed, on the condition that she took those days off when he was also off from work. Unfortunately, there was an issue where our father was supposed to have time off, but he got called back to work due to an emergency. We were devastated because it meant we would be back to square one. So, the responsibility fell on the neighbor again. He took advantage of the situation and subjected us to all forms of abuse - physical, mental, sexual, and emotional - with full force. When the nanny and our father came back, everything went back to normal. We occasionally spoke with our mother and other siblings, and we had told our mother that we wanted to come back and live with her and our other siblings. It was agreed that by the end of the school year, we would go live with them.

Within four months of living with us, our father noticed that the nanny was frequently going to the neighbor's apartment. When asked about it, she told our father that the neighbor was helping her with her computer programming course. Since she was an adult, our father didn't want to interfere too much. During those months, she started looking pale and throwing up a lot. We thought she was sick, but she made us promise not to tell our father. After a few weeks, she got better. We were happy that she had stopped throwing up because it had become overwhelming and disgusting. We noticed that our nanny stopped visiting the nice neighbor's apartment and started spending more time with her family in the neighboring city.

One day, our father called us and said he needed to talk to our nanny's family who lived there. We went with him, and to our surprise, the nanny came along with all her belongings. As young children, we didn't fully understand what was happening. Before going to the next town, we saw that our father had a falling out with the nice neighbor, and we assumed it had to do with how poorly he had treated us. Our father then told us not to go to the neighbor's apartment anymore, which made us incredibly happy but unable to express our true feelings.

When we arrived at the nanny's family's house, our father informed us that she would stay with her family. This news made us emotional because she had been kind to us, and her presence had greatly improved the neighbor's behavior towards us. As all of this was unfolding, the school year was coming to an end, and we were excited because our mother and other siblings were coming to spend time with us. We couldn't wait to leave and go stay with the rest of our family.

Encounter with Uncle's Boy

O ur little family reunion was short-lived but very memorable as we needed to return home with our mother to prepare for a new school year and new friends. I was the most excited because it meant that no longer would I have to endure the abuse. The school year went by quickly and was enjoyable as there was nothing to worry about except for the occasional nightmare that brought me to tears. However, whenever I saw a tall, dark-skinned man with a beard, my heart skipped a beat, as that was always the face of terror for me.

My mother thought I was being bullied at school because I was always scared to be by myself or go anywhere alone. I would jump whenever someone touched me or came too close to me. I became anti-people, except for immediate family members. It took me some time to warm up to people or make new friends as I feared that if I got too close, they would find out what had happened to me and cause trouble for my family with the "nice" neighbor, even though he lived several miles away from us. Every time I thought about my father, I also thought about the "nice" neighbor and what he would do to my father if he found out I had told anyone about his tricks.

Our long vacation was coming up, and we needed to decide where to spend it. One of my uncles invited us to spend part of the vacation with his family, and our father wanted us to stay with him. I was hesitant about going to our father's since he still lived in the same neighborhood as the "nice" neighbor, and I knew that there was a high chance we would run into each other. Although my entire family would be there, I didn't know what the "nice" neighbor could do. Therefore, I pleaded with my siblings to go to our uncle's house instead.

My uncle's wife adored me and would take me everywhere with her. She pleaded with my parents to let me stay longer, and I was ecstatic since that meant I wouldn't have to deal with the "nice" neighbor. My uncle had a houseboy who helped with house chores and other domestic work. Initially, he had an attitude towards me when we first got to my uncle's house. He would talk to everyone except me, and it made me wonder what I had done wrong. One day, my uncle took my other siblings out for sight-seeing and to shop for gifts, and I stayed back since I was tired. I was watching television in the living room when I heard someone clear their throat, and it was the houseboy. I didn't know what to say to him since he had barely talked to me, and it was concerning.

He asked if I would be willing to play a game with him, and I was ecstatic. We played games which helped me forget that my uncle and siblings were still not back. After playing several games, he asked if I had any games to play. I asked if we could play hide and seek, and he agreed. I went to hide, and he couldn't find me. When I finally came out from my hiding spot, he wasn't pleased that he had lost and that I refused to give away my hiding spot.

When it was my turn to hide again, he told me that if I hid in the same spot, I would lose the game. I agreed and decided to hide in the storage room this time. As I listened, I could hear the frustration in his voice as he repeatedly declared "found you" to an empty hiding spot. I felt a surge of excitement, realizing that I was much better at hiding than a high schooler. However, my excitement quickly turned to fear when I accidentally knocked over a broom, revealing my hiding spot. He became extremely angry and forcefully pushed me, causing me to fall onto a large bag of food. Terrified, I began to cry and begged him not to hurt me.

Suddenly, I saw the face of the "nice" neighbor in his expression as he covered my mouth and instructed me to be quiet. He proceeded to repeat the same actions that the neighbor had done the previous year. Before he could finish, we heard my uncle's car pull up and park outside. Startled, he quickly got off of me and warned that if I mentioned anything to anyone, he would ensure that I suffered even more. In that moment, I suppressed my cries, feeling a lump in my throat and aching in my chest.

He was the first to reach the door, pretending as if nothing had happened, and told my uncle that I had been crying because I missed my siblings. He claimed that he had been trying to console me, despite my continued tears. My uncle's wife overheard the conversation and questioned why I hadn't woken her up. He explained that he knew she was exhausted and wanted to let her sleep, thinking he could handle the situation alone. I stood there, observing everything and everyone as if I were watching a movie. I couldn't cry out or say anything, but tears kept streaming down my face from my bloodshot eyes. Eventually, the only words I managed to utter were to my immediate older sister, asking when we were supposed to leave.

During the remaining days of our stay before it was time to leave, I underwent a complete transformation. I became unusually quiet and would often find myself lost in my thoughts. I never disclosed what had happened to anyone, but I made a firm decision that I would never visit my uncle again as long as that house boy was living with him. I couldn't help but wonder if things would have been different if we had spent our vacation at my father's place, next to the "nice" neighbor.

As a new school year began, I continued to remain withdrawn and quiet, keeping to myself most of the time. Another year passed by, and now at the age of nine, I slowly started to open up to people. I began going outside and playing with other children, forming close friendships along the way. I even joined the girls' scout and started selling cookies and other sweet treats to our neighbors.

Encounter with the Generous Neighbor

I made a conscious decision to leave my trauma and nightmares behind me, determined to live like a normal girl without being haunted by my past experiences. I refused to let my past dictate my present or my future, instead choosing to bury those memories where they belonged - in the past.

As a member of the girl's scout, I actively participated in various charity work and volunteered to help in our community. Occasionally, we were given products to sell to our neighbors, with the proceeds going towards improving our community. We received boxes filled with cookies, candies, and popcorn, and were given a specific time frame for selling them. Meeting the deadline was crucial, as failure to do so meant having to pay for the products ourselves, which would hinder our progress within the girl's scout society.

Being naturally shy and not particularly skilled in sales, I knew it would take me some time to sell all my products. Luckily, one of my friends informed me about a kind and generous neighbor who would purchase the goods and distribute them to the children living in our neighborhood.

On that fateful day, we went to his building in the evening after he had returned from work. We explained to him what we were selling and shared that it was for a good cause. He carefully looked through the catalog, selecting several items that he wanted to purchase, and asked us to come back later. We were filled with excitement, knowing that we would be among the first to sell out based on the generous neighbor's order.

The following week, we returned to deliver the items he had purchased. He paid in full and expressed that we should visit again if we had more to sell. A few days later, while we were playing outside, he spotted me and asked me to accompany him to collect some of the cookies he had bought for the children in the neighborhood. Curious and unsuspecting, I went with him, and he ended up giving me almost all of the cookies. I happily distributed them to the other children I was playing with, and we joyfully shared and enjoyed them together.

When I arrived home, I excitedly told my mom about the generous neighbor and how kind he had been. She didn't think much of it but reminded me to be cautious and mindful of where I go, especially when alone. He had never shown any inappropriate interest in the children of the neighborhood, aside from occasionally giving out snacks. I never saw him as a predator because of his demeanor and the way he carried himself. He was in his late thirties and had a fiancé who was a college student. She would visit him frequently, making his true nature as a child abuser undetectable and unsuspected. Whenever his fiancé came around, everyone knew she was there. She was physically beautiful, well-mannered, and had a genuinely kind spirit. She made an effort to know everyone in the neighborhood by name and would stop to chat with people. She loved playing with the children in the neighborhood and would sometimes invite us to her apartment to play games.

For some reason, I became her favorite. She would come over to my house to visit. Whenever I told my mother that I was going to visit her, she did not question it because she knew that I would be safe. We usually knew when she was around, and that's when we would usually go to visit.

On that fateful weekend, she had told me that she would be there. I went over, thinking that she had arrived. When I knocked on the door, the generous neighbor answered and told me that she was on her way, and that I could come in and wait for her. Being a child and not thinking clearly, I went in to wait. I waited for about ten minutes but didn't see any sign of her. I got up and told him that I wanted to go home and would come back when she arrived. However, he insisted that I should wait longer and pulled me to the couch where he was sitting and watching television. Immediately, I sensed that something was not right. I told myself that if he attempted anything, I would scream and alert his neighbors.

Then, he started touching my legs and moving up to my thighs. I jolted, jumped up, and ran to the door, but it was locked. I started crying and pleading with him, promising that I wouldn't tell anyone about my encounter with him. However, it did not stop him from sticking his nasty finger in me. All I could think of was how to get out of there safely. I bent down and bit his arm, making sure that all my teeth penetrated through his skin. He screamed, pushed me off, and I started crying out loud. When he sensed that my sobbing might attract neighbors, he let me go. I couldn't go home right away; I had to hide, dry my face, and regain my composure before going home to avoid questions.

In the days that followed, I stayed at home, refusing to go outside and play. My mother thought that I was coming down with something. When his fiancé came and stayed the whole weekend without seeing me, she asked other children to tell me to come over and visit. Since I did not honor her invitation, she decided to come over to our house to check on me. I refused to see her, and that was how I retreated further into my shell, not wanting to interact with others to avoid anyone asking me questions and to avoid seeing the "generous neighbor."

A few months passed by, and I got sick. My mom took me to the hospital, and after the visit, I was prescribed some medications. When my mom took the prescription to the neighborhood pharmacy, the pharmacist there went through the medications with her. They discovered that one of the medications needed to be injected intramuscularly. The pharmacist, who was licensed to administer injections, offered to help with the injections.

Encounter with the Neighborhood Pharmacist

B eing sick and having to deal with seven days of antimalarial injections was no joke. These injections had to be given intramuscularly in the ventrogluteal site (buttocks), which meant that each day I went to the pharmacist for the injections, I had to partially expose my private area to him by pulling down my pants or raising my gown or skirt.

On the seventh day of the antimalarial injection, I went to get the shot by myself. I was feeling much better, and my sister, who would usually accompany me, had plans with her friends and couldn't come along. I didn't mind going alone because I had never had any issues with the pharmacist or the pharmacy technician. When I arrived, he was busy attending to many people picking up their prescriptions. He asked me to either wait for him to finish or go home and come back later. I decided to wait since I was still weak and didn't have the energy to go back and forth. It took a while for the place to clear out, and then it was finally my turn.

We entered the small room they used for patients' privacy when administering shots or any type of injection medication. I stood with my back towards him, waiting for him to draw the medication into the syringe. I felt him getting close to me, so I assumed he was ready to give me the shot. Just as I was about to pull my pants down, I felt his 'body part' rubbing against me. I jolted and moved away from him. He looked at me with his monstrous eyes and told me it would only take a minute and then it would be over. By then, tears were rolling down my face, and I was too shocked to run out of there. Suddenly, someone walked in and asked if anyone was there. I recognized the voice—it was my sister. I was filled with joy and gratitude that I had been saved by the bell.

He immediately zipped up his pants and asked them to give him a second. My tears started flowing even more. He gave me the injection and said I would need to follow up with him in a few days to ensure the medication was working. As soon as he administered the injection, I didn't wait for him to put a bandage on the site. I pulled up my pants and ran out. My sister was surprised when I rushed out, my face red and tears streaming down. She sensed that something was wrong and asked if he did anything to me. Of course, I denied it and told her it was just the shot, that this last one was more painful than the others. She knew I was lying and asked why it took so long for me to get the shot. I told her that when I arrived, the place was packed with so many people and he asked me to wait. She was furious and said she would talk to our mother about it because it wasn't right for him to make me wait while attending to others who arrived after me.

I cried the whole way home, thinking that there must be something wrong with me or something written on my forehead that makes all these men prey on me.

That night, I convinced myself that I was the cause of everything that had happened. I believed it was my fault that I always seemed to fall into the hands of these men. I couldn't eat that night, all I wanted was to close my eyes and never open them again. Throughout the night, I cried and prayed to God to take away this curse from me. I asked God to help me never get sick again, to avoid having to go to any doctor or pharmacist. From that day until my adulthood, I rarely told anyone when I was sick or injured.

I remember one time when I fell and had a laceration on my knee. I refused to tell anyone about it, risking infection. All I did was clean it with warm salt water until it eventually healed. It took longer than usual to completely heal, but I didn't care as long as I didn't have to go back to that pharmacist.

Throughout my teenage years, I tried my best to avoid boys. I kept to myself most of the time, except when I was at home with my family. I would always go to church and participate in various church activities. Everyone saw me as a very quiet and shy girl, but in reality, I was trying to avoid any interactions with men.

Teenage Life

B eing a teenager is never easy for some people, but for others, it seems to be a smooth journey. Unfortunately, it was never an easy life for me. I always tried to fit in, to belong, and to measure up to my peers. I constantly sought to please everyone, even if it meant inconveniencing or displeasing myself. I always aimed to do the right thing, as that's what I was taught. However, no matter how hard I tried to be good, my past would always haunt me, making me feel down and different from other teenagers. I didn't know how to cope with myself, so I dealt with it in my own way, which often involved isolating myself from others.

One of the things that brought me solace was spending time in church. We were born into a Christian family, and we continued practicing our faith as we grew up. We were taught that God was the best person to confide in about our problems, and that He would never fail us. Since I couldn't share my burden with anyone else, I decided to share it with God, hoping it would lighten the weight of my traumatic past.

I started attending every church activity at our local church. I joined various groups to keep my mind at ease, as my past abuse began to weigh heavily on me. If anyone was searching for me, they would always know where to find me: either at home, at school, or at church. It became my teenage lifestyle to the point where some people thought I was planning to become a nun.

Drawing closer to God and praying constantly helped me develop resilience against my abusers and oppressors, although the fear they instilled in me still lingered. I would never wish this kind of life, a life filled with fear, on anyone, not even my worst enemy. I would startle at every little noise around me, and my heart would skip a beat whenever a man approached. I avoided looking boys or men in the eyes when they spoke to me, so they wouldn't see the fear in my eyes. While it was a sign of respect in our culture to avoid direct eye contact with elders, I once got into trouble with my physical education teacher because I couldn't look at him while he spoke to me. However, that didn't change anything.

I also joined the church choir, although my voice was so soft and quiet that no one could hear me when I sang. But it didn't matter to me. I kept showing up for practices and performances. Knowing that I was a girl of few words, some people would sit next to me, hoping to engage me in conversation. One day, the choir had a performance at church. During our practice session for the song and a short drama, one of the pastors from the church came to watch us. I felt proud of myself because I performed well, and this pastor approached me to acknowledge it, despite knowing how shy I could be. I avoided looking at him, but he started talking to me about how God had given me the spirit of boldness instead of fear. His words resonated with me, as I had been fearful, especially around men, for a long time. He didn't say or do anything inappropriate, but he continued to offer empowering and encouraging words. He didn't invade my personal space or touch me, but he invited me to his office if I ever felt like talking about anything that was bothering me. I nodded my head and left, but I made up my mind not to confide in him because I feared he might use my story as an example, which would bring shame to my family. Nevertheless, his words did help alleviate some of my fear.

Speaking of church, men of God, and pastors, when I was about fifteen years old, despite my efforts to avoid men and boys, a pastor (not from our church) came to our house for a family prayer. This pastor worked with my mother and provided counseling services at their workplace. He convinced my mother that we needed a family prayer session. So, she invited him over on a weekend. Unfortunately, he chose to visit on a Saturday afternoon, when we were resting from our weekend chores. Usually, my mother would assign us our Saturday chores on Friday nights to prepare us for the tasks ahead. We used to have Saturday afternoons as our family time together, but not on this particular Saturday.

We exchanged pleasantries with the pastor, and he began praying after we all gathered in our living room. During the prayer, he claimed to see things in the spiritual realm. He told my mother that I was possessed by a spirit that needed to be cast out, as it would hinder my blessings and delay my achievements in life.

Of course, I possessed all the characteristics that, according to him, indicated someone being possessed by a marine spirit. Apparently, if you were beautiful and kept to yourself, it was believed that you had a spirit possessing you. My mother, trusting the man of God and not wanting her child to miss out on any blessings or be hindered in any way, panicked and became disturbed. Innocently, she asked what could be done to prevent this from happening.

Encounter with a Man of God

My family and I have always been devoted Christians, striving to follow God's words and commandments and to do good to others. We had a regular prayer routine, coming together to pray in the mornings and at night. We thanked Him for waking us up in the mornings, asked for His provisions and protections throughout the day, and expressed gratitude at night for His presence and asked for His continued protection throughout the night. Occasionally, we would also engage in fasting as part of our spiritual practice. It was our established routine.

However, when this man of God prophesied about the presence of an unknown spirit within me, everything changed. I was sentenced to fourteen days of fasting and praying. Initially, I was supposed to meet with the pastor every evening at his office. However, due to my involvement in extracurricular activities scheduled for the evenings, we reached an agreement that I would attend the closing prayers every three days instead. The first few days of fasting and prayers went smoothly. I would fast until noon and then go to the pastor's office in the evening for prayers.

Before I continue, let me provide some background information about this man of God. He was married and had children, some of whom were older than me, while others were around the same age. It is important to note that this self-proclaimed man of God was in his early to mid-fifties, while I was just fifteen years old at the time.

On the tenth day of fasting, when I arrived at his office, the man of God was counseling someone, so I waited outside. Once he was finished, he called me in. Before we began our prayers for the day, he took out a bottle of anointed oil and explained that it was blessed. He told me that he would apply it to me during our prayers. I didn't have any issues with this, as I had used anointed oil and holy water in extensive prayers before. He prayed for about ten minutes and then started applying the oil to me, starting from my head and working his way down. He applied some to my arms, and then he pulled up my dress (I was wearing a below the knee dress).

At that moment, I froze and tried to pull my dress back down, as I didn't think getting partially undressed was part of the prayer session. However, he continued praying and held my hand with his free hand, telling me to stop fighting the spirit. He proceeded to apply the anointed oil from my thigh down to my feet. While he was applying the oil, his hand reached my underwear. As soon as I felt his hand near my private area, my heart skipped a beat, adrenaline started pumping, and I was ready to run out of there. I believed that he must have sensed my fear and decided not to proceed with whatever he had planned. I had one more session with him remaining.

Two days before my last day of fasting (the twelfth day), he spoke to my mother and reassured her that the prayers were going well. He explained that the final day would involve a spiritual bath, where he would bathe me with holy water and anointed oil. He asked me to bring a towel with me.

When the day arrived, I was too scared to go alone, so I asked my sister to accompany me. My sister was around seventeen years old, but she was a fighter and very stubborn. She would challenge anyone, regardless of their age. When the man of God saw that I had come with my sister, his demeanor changed. He could sense that something was amiss. He didn't know if I had said anything to my sister.

Upon entering his office, he informed us that he would say a general prayer for both of us, after which my sister should wait outside while he concluded my prayers with me. I asked him why my sister couldn't be present during the concluding prayer. He explained that there was a possibility of the spirit he was trying to cast out of me transferring to my sister and possessing her, which would not be favorable. This meant that my sister would have to go through the same process I was going through - fourteen days of fasting and prayer. My sister saw the terror in my eyes, and she held my hand, assuring me that she would be just outside the door.

With tears in my eyes, I gave her a nod. We were in no position to challenge a man of God.

As soon as my sister left his office, he asked me if I had brought a towel. I nodded in affirmation. He instructed me to remove everything I was wearing, including my underwear, and wrap the towel around myself. He left the office, saying he would return in five minutes to give me time to undress and gather the necessary items for the prayers. I followed his instructions, but my interest in the prayer had waned. Instead, I was preoccupied with planning how to defend myself if he tried anything.

When he returned to his office, I was prepared, clad only in the tightly wrapped towel around my small, naked body. He asked me to kneel in front of him, and he began singing praises to God. With his right hand on my forehead, he continued praying. I kept my eyes closed as instructed but periodically opened one eye to ensure my safety. I noticed that as the intensity of the prayer increased, he would push or pull me, causing me to sway back and forth.

The prayer seemed to go on longer than the previous ones, and at one point, he began speaking in different tongues. He slowed his pace and started sprinkling holy water on me. Opening a bottle of anointed oil, he poured it onto my head, allowing it to trickle down my face and onto other parts of my body. My body jerked when he forcefully removed my towel and began rubbing the oil onto my skin. I was on high alert, ready for fight or flight.

He knelt beside me while continuing to rub in the oil. As he reached my chest, his hands cupped my developing breasts, and his entire body pressed against mine, his hardness touching me. The burning sensation of the oil in my eyes, coupled with the anger and strength I had stored up, propelled me to push him away. He stumbled backward, knocking over a lamp on a nearby table.

I quickly stood up, grabbed the towel to cover my body, collected my clothes, and rushed into the bathroom within his office. There, I used the towel to wipe off the oil from my skin and got dressed. When I opened the bathroom door, I made a beeline for the exit, unlocking it and stepping outside. I saw my sister approaching the door, drawn by the sound of the falling lamp. She asked if everything was alright, and I assured her that we were finished and needed to leave.

The so-called man of God pretended as if nothing had happened, explaining to his wife, who had rushed to the office, that I had accidentally knocked over the lamp during the deliverance. I felt a sense of pride and empowerment, realizing that I could fight my own battles without relying on anyone else. My sister, however, had a gut feeling that something had occurred in that office, and she persisted in asking me for details. I continued to deny anything had happened, but I questioned her if she had ever experienced a one-on-one prayer with this pastor. She responded that she had never and would never do so. She had never placed her trust in most of these self-proclaimed prophets and supposed men of God. That experience marked the end of my engagement in one-on-one sessions with pastors or men of God.

Admirer #1

I grew up to become a beautiful, well-behaved, and down-to-earth young girl (I'm not trying to boast, but to acknowledge God's artwork in creating me). As a young girl, I had admirers just like other girls my age. I vividly remember two of them whom I did not realize genuinely and innocently loved me, but I never gave them any opportunity to come close.

I had a nationwide examination for high schoolers coming up and needed extramural classes to be well-prepared. During those classes, there was a young boy who would always sit directly behind me. Interestingly, we attended the same church but had never exchanged a word. It took me a few weeks to notice that he consistently chose the seat behind me. You see, I have a tendency to keep to myself, even when I'm in the midst of friends, I rarely express myself. Some people who knew me then would describe me as a shy young girl. I kind of agree with them, but part of my reserved nature stemmed from the trauma I had suffered.

During the last week of the extramural classes, he approached me to introduce himself and see if he could get me to chat with him. He was popular, lively, and had a lot of friends. It was his excitable behavior that caught my attention the first time I noticed him in that class. He introduced himself and asked if I lived around there because many people in the class came from different streets and backgrounds. I told him where I lived, and he mentioned that we lived in the same city, which was not news to me since I knew where he lived. His younger sister was in the same Girl Scout society. I told him that we went to the same church, and he mentioned that he had never seen me there. He noticed me on the first day of the extramural class but didn't know how to approach me because I tended to keep to myself and barely talked to anyone except for the head instructor at the center. I mentioned that the head instructor lived next to me and had convinced my parents to let me take the class to help with my examination preparation.

Afterward, he started coming to my house to visit me and would also approach me at church to see how I was doing. During his initial visit, I thought he was just passing by and wanted to say hi, but he kept showing up at my house. Over time, I went from feeling uncomfortable with him coming over to being okay with it. We would talk about the colleges we applied to and our reasons for choosing them, as well as the appropriate courses of study.

A few months later, we both received admissions to different universities in different states. I thought it would be the end of our friendship, but it didn't stop him. Whenever he was in town, he would come over to my house to visit, and it was always enjoyable to have him around. My parents usually didn't allow male friends in the house, but for some reason, he was always welcomed and became well-known to the whole family.

One day, during one of his visits, he tried to kiss me. I pulled away and told him that I don't kiss because it gives me a bacterial attack in my mouth. How I came up with that, I have no idea, but it worked. It worked for a year, but the following year he had to move to a different country, and we lost contact.

Admirer #2

This second admirer was not just an admirer, but a suitor. One of my aunties was married into his family. He, along with his siblings and cousins, would come with my auntie whenever she was visiting. So, we practically grew up together because we would also visit them to see my auntie. When we were little, he was incredibly overprotective of me. He would fight and attack anyone who came looking for trouble with me. Initially, I despised him because he seemed like trouble himself. However, I didn't realize that most of his fights were because of me. Whether he heard someone say something bad about me or saw someone do something bad to me, he would always be there, making sure I was okay.

I was a very shy girl growing up, so whenever he approached me with care and concern, I felt embarrassed. I hated it when people would look at us and say that we would end up getting married to each other.

After graduating from high school, I had already planned which college to attend. I didn't bother telling him since he lived in a different state. I remember one fateful day when I was at home with my siblings and he came to our house, wanting to talk to me. He showed me his passport, which he had just picked up, and informed me that his father was making plans to send him abroad. His father was well-off and would do anything to ensure that all his children were well-established.

He explained that the reason he came to show me the travel documents was to ask me to marry him and give him some time to establish himself overseas before coming back for me. I laughed and told him that we were too young to be thinking about marriage. I said that we should be more focused on choosing a college and planning for our futures after college. He asked me to promise not to marry someone else until he was ready. We were both very young, in our teenage years. So, I told him that I couldn't make a promise like that because I might not be able to keep it. I advised him to go ahead with his plans to travel since his father had already made arrangements. I encouraged him to live his life, and I would live mine. If by chance we were meant to be together, we would find each other again.

I didn't realize that he didn't take my refusal and advice well until about a year later when my aunt came to visit us. She asked if he had been in contact with me, and I simply said no and walked away. My aunt was much older than me, and I didn't feel comfortable discussing relationship matters with her, out of respect.

Later in the week, my aunt came to see me and asked to speak with me privately. She took me to the guest room and began discussing Alex (Admirer #2) with me. She told me that after I declined his proposal, stating that we should focus on college rather than marriage, he went home and told her the reason for my refusal. According to him, I declined because he was young and didn't have his own money. He informed my aunt that he would no longer travel abroad but instead stay back, work hard, and come back to propose again. He wanted to prove to me how much he loved me and how well he could take care of me if I accepted his marriage proposal. My aunt mentioned that every time they crossed paths, he would inquire about me and my marital status before anything else.

During my second year of college, he began reaching out to me again. Being a principled person, I decided to be kind and be friends with him. He started visiting my parents' house more frequently. Of course, the whole family knew him through my aunt, and they were aware of his deep affection for me when we were younger. However, they were not aware of his previous proposal to me.

After several years of growing closer to me and my family, and getting to know me better, he proposed once again. Once again, I declined. He was hurt because he believed that now that he had acquired wealth and properties and was financially well-off, I would accept his proposal. I explained to him that I had declined his proposal when we were younger because we simply weren't ready for marriage, not because of his financial situation. I told him that even now, his wealth would not change my decision. If I were to accept his proposal at this point, people would assume that I was a gold digger who initially refused because he wasn't wealthy enough, only to accept when he became well-off.

He was persistent for a while because it's unusual for a young girl to decline an offer and proposal, especially from a handsome young man who seemed to have everything a woman could want. He believed that his persistence would eventually lead to him getting what he desired. In the years that followed, he continued to visit consistently. However, when he discovered that I had a boyfriend, he realized that I truly meant it when I told him that we wouldn't work as a couple. He wasn't happy about it, as I had anticipated, but he eventually moved on and found himself a girlfriend whom he eventually married.

He stayed in touch for a few months after that, but eventually, he completely moved on from our past connection.

Encounter with Boyfriend #1

My encounter with the so-called man of God made me feel as though I was cursed, destined to be sexually abused by men. However, it also helped prepare me to face the challenges of the world ahead. Throughout my teenage years, I trained myself to fight against evil men at all times.

One day, while taking a bus ride from a friend's house, I had an incident that further fueled my frustration with men taking advantage of my innocence. I was about eighteen years old and exhausted from enduring such mistreatment. The bus was crowded, with standing passengers packed tightly together. I greeted the passengers around me in a polite manner, unaware that this would invite evil into my life.

There was a male passenger behind me who was essentially leaning on me. At first, I didn't pay much attention to his actions. I moved forward slightly, hoping to create some space, but to my dismay, he moved forward with me, still pressing against me. I could feel him rubbing against me, but I initially thought it was due to the bus's movements. However, the intensity of his actions increased. Whenever I moved, he moved with me. It was then that I turned around and saw that he had exposed himself.

I confronted him, asking what he was doing.

In response, he told me to be quiet, claiming that I was complaining because he hadn't paid me. I asked him to repeat himself, as if to confirm what I had just heard. Something within me shifted when I tightly grasped the collar of his shirt and demanded that he pay me for what he had done. The commotion attracted the attention of other passengers, and I was relieved because I knew that I had people standing up for me.

I explained to the other passengers what he had done and what he had said to me. As a result, he received the beating of his life and was ultimately kicked off the bus. Although I felt embarrassed by the ordeal, I was grateful to have others supporting me and taking action against the man's despicable behavior.

I was about twenty-two years old when I found myself in a relationship. It wasn't something I truly desired, but I wanted to fit in and appear normal among my peers. I took my time to carefully select someone whom I believed would be the right match for me. I turned down numerous dates out of fear of falling into the arms of an abuser, until I met this guy.

He lived in a city away from mine, and we met when he visited his cousin who happened to be our neighbors. He was five years older than me and, to be honest, not particularly attractive. He was an okay-looking guy, of average height, though I had hoped for someone taller. He had a slight air of self-importance and a touch of selfishness. Despite his flaws, I decided to give him a chance, thinking that his lack of the qualities I expected in a partner might humble him a bit.

It wasn't until I met him that I realized the extent of the damage and trauma I had been carrying within me. It took about four months and three dates before I could allow him to hug me without feeling as though I was being abused by another predator. I didn't share my story with him out of fear that he might not want anything to do with me.

Around six months into our relationship, he began growing impatient with me. During one of our dates, he attempted to kiss me, but I froze and tried to push him away. Concerned, he asked if everything was alright. I made up an excuse, claiming that I was coming down with a cold and didn't want him to get sick as well. He believed that my hesitation stemmed from shyness and thought I needed more time to open up to him. When he discovered that he was my first "official" boyfriend, he decided to be patient and give us more time to get to know each other better.

However, as time passed, his patience started to wear thin. I couldn't blame him, as it was taking me a long time to feel comfortable and open up to him, despite my genuine liking for him. His reputation and ego were on the line, adding to the pressure and strain on our relationship.

I couldn't stop thinking about it, contemplating what would happen to our relationship if things didn't go well, as I had developed deep feelings for him. It was his birthday, and I thought the perfect gift would be to let him sleep with me. I surprised him by showing up at his house after his friends had left, and I allowed him to kiss me. However, when he began touching me, I froze. I couldn't move. I lay there, trapped in my thoughts, blaming myself for bringing this curse upon myself. I felt foolish for thinking that not all men were the same, as it felt like he was violating me.

On my way home, tears streamed down my face, regretting my decision to let him touch me. I retreated into my shell, shutting out everyone and refusing to talk about it. My sister, who was rarely home due to her job, noticed the unbearable silence that had taken over the house. She observed that I had stopped talking about my boyfriend and would quickly change the subject whenever he was mentioned.

He made several attempts to be intimate with me after that first time, but I always had an excuse ready, because in my mind, I had lumped him into the category of predators. On one occasion, he came to my house and one of my siblings let him in, aware of our relationship. To avoid any awkwardness and unwanted questions, I sat with him in the living room. We engaged in conversation, but I tried my best to avoid looking at him, as every time I did, anger surged within me.

This had been going on since his birthday. Whenever thoughts of him or what had happened crossed my mind, I felt a mix of anger, fury, resentment, and guilt all at once.

He reached out and held my hand. I pulled away, but he held on tightly with both hands. He expressed his love for me and asked if he had hurt me in any way. With tears in my eyes, I looked at him and pulled away, telling him that I wasn't hurt. We sat in silence for a while, with him occasionally staring at me, before he eventually decided to leave.

As he left, I knew that it marked the end of our relationship. Looking back now, I realize that I didn't trust him enough to share my story with him. Despite his ego and arrogance, he made several attempts to bring us back to where we were before. However, I couldn't return to feeling free around him, especially after overhearing him tell one of his friends that I was always seeking attention, as if I had won some kind of beauty pageant.

When he realized that nothing was changing between us, he decided it was time for us to move on with our lives. He couldn't bring himself to tell me in person, so he sent me a "Good luck" card along with an extensive letter explaining why we needed to go our separate ways.

A few months after our "break-up," for which I partly blame myself due to my self-isolation from him (a decision I have no regrets about), I landed a good job and moved to a different state.

There, I found true happiness and peace within myself.

Encounter with Boyfriend #2

In my language, there's a saying that when a girl outgrows the question "whose daughter is this?", she moves on to the question "whose wife is this?". At this point in my life, many of my friends were either getting married or engaged, while I remained single with no intentions of involving myself with any man. I had convinced myself that to be in a successful relationship, as a woman, I needed to be willing to sacrifice everything and be ready to fulfill any sexual demands. This distorted belief was a result of the extensive damage I had endured from multiple instances of abuse.

One day, while watching a movie about a young girl who had been shuffled from one foster home to another, I came across a scene that struck a chord with me. The girl was facing bullying at school and began skipping classes as a result. When her elderly African American foster mother discovered her truancy, she wanted to punish the girl. However, the young girl defiantly responded that there was no point in going to school because she already knew that the only thing she would be good at was opening her legs. When asked where she learned such a notion, she revealed that it was her previous foster mother who had instilled this belief in her. The phrase "only be good at opening her legs" lingered in my mind, and I found myself repeatedly questioning if this applied to me. I carried this burden for a long time, feeling trapped by this belief.

After about a year of rejecting proposals for friendship or marriage, I reached a point where I didn't want to remain single anymore. I made the decision to give relationships a try. An opportunity arose for me to travel abroad, and I was filled with happiness at the prospect of leaving my past behind and starting a new life. Things went well for several months as I began working and fell in love with my job.

A few months into my new job, my employer decided to send me and some colleagues on a work-related training in a different city. During the training, we were divided into different groups to facilitate the instructors' teaching. The first instructor in my group was an attractive, tall man who spoke eloquently and effortlessly commanded attention. As the days went by, we listened to other instructors give their lectures.

At the end of one class, as we were leaving the training center, I noticed that the instructor from the first day was right behind me. He asked me how I found his lecture. Initially, I didn't realize he was addressing me because I preferred to remain invisible, avoiding being noticed. I continued walking until he called my name. Surprised, I turned around and greeted him. He mentioned that he had been wondering if I enjoyed his lecture since

I appeared disinterested. We started discussing the topic he had taught, and I began asking him questions about it. He seemed taken aback, mentioning that he had expected me or someone else to ask those questions during class. We stood and conversed about the lecture for almost thirty minutes before he asked if I wanted to grab a drink. I declined, stating that I didn't drink and needed to go home. In truth, I was trying to distance myself from him. He asked if it would be alright for him to call me and requested my phone number. I hesitated but eventually gave it to him. Throughout the remainder of the training, he didn't call or bother me, though I did my best to avoid him.

On the last day of the training, one of the administrative staff members arranged for all of us, including the instructors, to go out and eat. When we arrived at the restaurant, he signaled to me that he had saved a seat next to him. Not wanting to be impolite, I went and sat beside him. Despite his efforts to keep the conversation going, I only responded with a side smile or a nod.

After the outing, as people started to leave, he noticed that I was getting ready to go and asked if it would be alright for us to grab drinks sometime when I had the time. I reminded him that I didn't drink, so he suggested coffee or tea instead. I accepted his offer, and he mentioned that he would call or text me to plan a day that worked for both of us.

We progressed from meeting for coffee or

tea to seeing each other more frequently. We enjoyed each other's company and found that we had a lot to talk about, which made us believe we had many things in common. Things were going well for several months until he started getting too close. I knew that a day like this would come, but it still caught me off guard. I felt tension on my side because I didn't know how to react. Whenever I get close to a man, terrible memories flood my mind, causing me to withdraw and become tense. Sometimes I freeze, sometimes I shake. This time, I froze.

He sensed that something was wrong and asked if I was okay, but I simply nodded. I kept telling myself to just open my legs because that was the only thing I was good at – no emotions, no feelings. I lay there and let him take advantage of me. When he was done, I got up, cleaned myself up, got dressed, and left without saying a word to him. He tried to talk to me, thinking that I might be shy or feeling guilty about what had happened. I suppose he was shocked to discover that I had left. He made several attempts to call me and find out what had happened, but I refused to answer or return his calls.

Third is a Charm Like They Say

After working for the company that sent us to the training, where I met boyfriend #2, for two years, I received a significant promotion that required me to relocate to a different city. It was a great opportunity, and I needed to leave that city, so I accepted the offer. Upon arriving in the new city, I continued minding my own business and keeping to myself, except for the occasional greetings and interactions with those who spoke to me.

There was a guy who worked in a building close to my workplace. We would often run into each other during lunch breaks. He was incredibly handsome, soft-spoken, humble, and reserved. He was one of those people who you couldn't help but notice, even if you were blind. Prior to our first encounter, I had already heard my colleagues talking about him. Some described him as rude, others said he was arrogant, mean, or shy. However, I didn't pay much attention, as I had little to no interest in discussing men or people in general.

The first time we crossed paths, I noticed that he glanced at me. Honestly, I was also looking at him to see if he was the same person my colleagues had been talking about. I didn't know that he would be getting his own lunch, as he had his own company. Based on what my colleagues had mentioned, he was worth quite a bit of money or, I should say, valuable. He should have people assigned to tasks like fetching his lunch.

On the few occasions that we ran into each other, we both pretended not to see or acknowledge each other. It started to seem like one of us was stalking the other, and it no longer felt like a coincidence. So, I decided to change my routine. Over the next two days, I either brought food from home, snacked on things, or went for lunch after everyone else had finished.

After a week, I returned to the lunch spot, and there he was, wearing a big smile. I looked behind me to confirm that the smile was directed at me before smiling back, as I didn't want to embarrass myself. You know, it's like waving back at someone who is waving at someone behind you, and then realizing the wave wasn't for you, so you pretend you were just scratching your hair.

Anyways, getting back to my story. So, when I smiled back, he stood there and waited until I got close to where he was standing before he started speaking. He greeted me and mentioned that he had been wondering what had happened to me because I had missed lunch for a week. I smiled and lied, saying that I had been out of town. He smiled back but gave me a look that exposed my lie. He said, "Oh, for some reason, I thought I saw you leaving yesterday, and the day before that, and the other day as well." I couldn't help but burst into laughter and told him that I didn't realize I was being investigated. He laughed too, extended his hand for a handshake, and introduced himself as Darren. I reciprocated and told him my name as well.

Interestingly, he never mentioned that he was the owner of the company next to where I work; he simply said that he worked over there. Curiosity got the better of me, so I asked him about the nature of their business. He proceeded to give me a long explanation of what type of business they were involved in. I was amazed and commented on how much he seemed to know about the company, almost as if he owned it. However, he refrained from making any further comment on that and changed the topic. He advised me not to starve myself or skip lunch just to avoid him. I smiled and assured him that there was no such thing, as I brought my own lunch from home.

Little did I know that my statement would get me into trouble. He then asked if I could bring him lunch from home as well, mentioning that it would be greatly appreciated. My brain went blank, and I just stared at him, completely caught off guard. Sensing my confusion, he quickly clarified that he was just messing with me. By that time, our food orders were ready, and we bid each other goodbye. As he turned around, he mentioned that it was nice to meet me and that he was looking forward to that lunch from home. My heart started beating faster than normal, and I couldn't help but smile and say, "Likewise." I didn't know where that response came from, as I immediately wanted to take it back, but it was already out there, just like a loud fart. LOL.

After he left, I walked over to the cashier to pay for my food. The cashier remarked that he must have liked me because she had never seen him speak to anyone, let alone engage in a conversation. I simply smiled and left. In the following weeks, I made a conscious effort to avoid him as much as possible, as I already had a feeling that it might end up like my previous relationships.

One day, a colleague approached me and asked if there was something going on between the handsome guy and me. He mentioned that the cashier had seen us chatting on another occasion. I responded by telling him that we had simply had a conversation and that it was none of his business. I noticed that some people at work were already talking about it, but this guy was the only one brave enough to ask me directly. The office gossip only served to exacerbate the situation and made me even more determined to stay away from him.

I was starting to forget about him, but then one day, I found myself leaving the office late due to an impending deadline. As I walked towards my vehicle, I heard a familiar voice from a passing car say, "Hello, stranger!" I knew it was him because our office buildings shared the same parking deck. I stopped, turned around, and greeted him back with a forced smile. He remarked that if he didn't know any better, he would say I had been avoiding him. I quickly denied it, explaining that I had been extremely busy. He had a way with words, so he mentioned that he thought I had been scared away when he asked me to bring him homemade lunch. He then confidently declared that he would be the one to bring me homemade food. I laughed and teasingly said, "Like you know how to light a stove, let alone cook." He assured me that he would surprise me.

Feeling exhausted and not in the mood for a lengthy conversation, I faked a yawn. He assured me that he wouldn't keep me any longer but mentioned that he would bring me lunch the next day since I often worked late and might not have time to cook when I got home. Grateful, I thanked him and insisted that he didn't need to buy me lunch, as I could afford to buy my own. However, he shook his head and clarified that he wasn't going to buy me lunch but make one for me. I chuckled mockingly, telling him that we would see. As I was about to leave, he surprised me by asking for my phone number. He explained that he wanted to alert me when he brought the lunch. I hesitated for a moment but eventually gave it to him. I then walked towards my car, noticing that he remained there until I drove off before leaving himself.

As soon as I walked through my door, I received a text message from him, checking to see if I had made it home safely. I replied, assuring him that I was safe and hoping that he had also arrived home without any issues. We exchanged messages for a while before finally saying our goodnights. I made a conscious effort to avoid asking intimate or overly personal questions.

Throughout the night, thoughts of him consumed my mind, and I found myself wondering what he could possibly want from me. I couldn't shake off the remarks made by the cashier and my colleagues at work about how he rarely engaged in conversations with anyone. I kept questioning whether he was married, had children, was divorced, a widower, or had a girlfriend. With all these thoughts swirling in my head, sleep eluded me. I tossed and turned throughout the night, unable to find rest. I couldn't even remember if I had managed to sleep at all, but as soon as my alarm rang, I forced myself to get up and start preparing for work.

While at work, my concentration wasn't as focused as usual. I found myself constantly glancing at my phone, hoping to receive a text from him. That morning, after finishing my presentation, I had a bit of free time before lunch, so I decided to confide in my sister about my feelings for this man. My sister, who was unaware of my past abuse, listened to everything I had to say and responded with a simple "oh, okay." I became frustrated with her lack of probing questions or deeper concern. To make matters worse, she mentioned that she had heard similar stories from me before. I was about to end our conversation when I received a message notifying me that I was needed in the conference room. I quickly ended the call with my sister, grabbed my notepad and pen, and headed straight to the conference room without even checking my calendar to see if there was a scheduled meeting at that time.

When I entered the conference room, I noticed that it was empty except for one person sitting at the end of the table. As I approached, I realized it was HIM. My entire body felt weak, and I nearly stumbled. I was so confused and stunned that I couldn't utter a single word. I noticed that my mouth was hanging open, but no words came out. I couldn't believe he had shown up at my workplace without informing me beforehand. This was the same person who had texted me throughout the previous night but hadn't sent a single message in the morning.

When I didn't hear from him that morning, my mind started to jump to the worst conclusions. I thought maybe he wasn't interested in me, maybe he was unavailable, or perhaps he had realized that talking to me was a mistake. After about a minute of standing there in a state of confusion, I managed to ask the first two questions that came to mind: "What are you doing here?" and "How did you get in here?" He chuckled and replied that he knew his way around. I was still standing there, feeling bewildered, when he walked up to me and handed me a bag, saying that he had brought me lunch as promised. I opened my mouth to protest, but he quickly added that he had noticed how busy I was and knew I wouldn't have time to make my own lunch. I smiled and expressed my gratitude for his kind gesture. He wanted to stay longer and chat, but I was in a rush to return to my office. I hurriedly entered my office, placed the food on my desk, and still couldn't fully comprehend what had just happened. I was still waiting for an answer about how he had gained access to the conference room when my phone chimed. He had sent me a text, telling me to enjoy my meal and adding a smiley face emoji. I panicked and ignored his text for an entire week, hoping it would make him stop texting or searching for me.

The following week, I was in my small office when my boss knocked on the door and entered, taking a seat. I observed that he didn't have any folders with him, suggesting that he wasn't there for an official business matter. He asked me what was going on with me, and I replied that there was nothing significant happening except for my efforts to finish up my report for the day. He clarified that he wasn't referring to work, but rather my personal life. He inquired about how my weekend had been and how my week was progressing so far. I wasn't sure where he was heading with these questions. If I didn't know him well, I might have assumed he was trying to flirt with me. We conversed for about ten minutes when his cellphone rang. I felt relieved, assuming he would leave my office to take the call. However, he remained seated and answered it. Thinking he needed privacy, I stood up, but he signaled for me to stay. I pretended to read some reports on my desktop computer, attempting to return to the task I had been working on before he entered my office. However, I couldn't concentrate. I started feeling increasingly uncomfortable when he said, "Hold on a minute, she's here with me," and extended his arm to hand me the phone. I couldn't comprehend what was happening. I couldn't recall us having a mutual friend aside from his wife, and I knew he was speaking to a male friend, not his wife. I greeted the person on the other end of the line and heard a very familiar voice saying to me, "You're finally talking to me. I almost forgot what you sound like." I froze in my seat, my heart pounding as if it would burst out of my chest. Instantly, I blushed and felt as though I might faint. I managed to regain my composure, cleared my throat, and asked who I was speaking to. My boss stood up to leave my office, so I asked him to wait so I could return his phone. He smiled at me and said, "Take your time. I'll come back for my phone when you're done talking to him," then walked out of my office. I was utterly confused and found myself asking, "What just happened?" I tried to wrap my head around the situation when the voice on the phone asked if I was still there. I responded by asking, "How do you know Eric?"

So, it turns out that my boss was playing matchmaker for Darren and me without my knowledge. He had been the one giving Darren information about my schedule, such as when I leave for lunch or for the day. He had asked Darren to bring lunch to the conference room and arranged for me to be there. All along, it was my boss orchestrating everything, and I had been under the impression that I was special, the only one Darren talked to at our workplace.

As I held the phone, listening to Darren speak, I wasn't really paying attention to what he was saying. Instead, I was trying to sort out my feelings. I didn't know if I should be angry, furious, happy, or excited that he had called. His deep voice snapped me out of my thoughts, asking if I had been listening to him. I said yes, but in reality, I hadn't heard a single word. I pretended to understand what he had proposed, even though I didn't. So, he asked what I thought about it. I stumbled a bit and asked him to clarify what he meant.

Honestly, I didn't hear a single word that he said, but I pretended as if I had, even though I didn't understand what he was asking me. So, he said, "What don't you understand? I mean, like going out on a date. Or don't you go on dates?" I assured him that I knew what going on a date meant because I had been on many, but I wanted clarification on what he meant by "going out to eat." I agreed to go on a date with him that weekend, and he said he would text me to let me know when he would pick me up. Just as I was about to ask him, "Pick me up from where?" he abruptly said, "Talk to you later," and hung up the phone.

I took my boss's phone to his office to return it and to confront him about what he had done. When I arrived at his office, he was already on another call. He gestured for me to place the phone on his table. I did as he asked, but before I could ask any questions, he silently mouthed that he would talk to me later. Throughout that day and the following day, he avoided me like the plague. It was clear that he didn't want to answer any of my questions, knowing that I had a lot of them for him.

The next day after the phone encounter with "him," I received a text message from him, informing me of the time he would pick me up for our date that weekend. On the designated day, he had already made a reservation at a fancy restaurant, but he refused to disclose its location to me. He arrived at my apartment and called to let me know that he was waiting outside. Since I was already dressed, I grabbed my purse and went to meet him.

To my surprise, he had a small sign with the words, "Would you please be my date tonight?" It seemed like he was either trying to be funny or unsure if I would recognize him. I glanced around, making sure none of my neighbors were watching, before taking the sign from him. As I was about to open the car door and get in, he stopped me and opened the passenger door for me. It was a thoughtful gesture.

The outing turned out to be enjoyable. I discovered a different side of him - funny, playful, and humble. It was during this date that I learned about his friendship with my boss. It was my boss who had orchestrated all those coincidental encounters we had been experiencing. They had been best friends since middle school, attending the same middle and high schools, and even the same college. After college, they initially planned to pursue their business ventures together but ended up going their separate ways. They had intended to get married in the same year, but Darren's long-time girlfriend broke his heart by leaving him for another man. This devastating experience led him to shy away from deep relationships.

He proceeded to share with me how he reacted when he first laid eyes on me. He had a scheduled meeting with my boss at his office. However, when my boss didn't show up and wasn't answering his phone, he decided to come over and see what was going on. He claimed that he saw me emerging from Eric's office, holding a stack of files. At the time, he didn't know who I was, but he instantly felt drawn to me. Curious, he asked Eric about my identity and why he hadn't shown up for their meeting. Eric explained that I was new and he was in the process of acquainting me with the office routine. Playfully, he said to Eric, "What office routine? I don't recall you showing any of the other staff members an office routine." They shared a laugh, and Eric told him that I was special. They discussed business matters, and as he was about to leave, Eric mentioned that he should consider giving love another chance. He brushed it off and prepared to depart when Eric suggested that he could set us up. He smiled and left the conversation at that.

According to him, Eric would not stop talking about me whenever they spent time together. Eric would mention seeing me go to the little shop across the street to buy my lunch. He kept planting the idea in his mind until he finally went to that shop on the day we officially met. He also revealed that when he saw me leaving late from the parking lot one evening, it was Eric who informed him that I had been working late. As he recounted these details, it became clear to me that all those coincidental encounters were not coincidental at all. They had been planned. He expressed that on the day he saw me at the shop, he understood what Eric meant when he described me as special. He instantly felt a liking towards me and hoped that I was single.

That explained why Eric had invited me to his house one weekend and told me I could bring my boyfriend or fiancé along. Little did I know, he was testing me. I honestly informed him that I didn't have either, but unfortunately, I couldn't make it that weekend due to a prior arrangement. That gave him the response he was seeking without any effort on his part.

Aside from the arranged meetings orchestrated by my boss, Darren and I had plenty to talk about. We found ourselves engrossed in conversation, losing track of time as we sipped our drinks and chatted away. However, as we were preparing to leave, something shifted. When we reached the door, he placed his hand on my back to guide me out, but I instinctively pulled away and fell silent. Confusion washed over him as he tried to comprehend what had just happened.

Throughout the drive home, I remained quiet. He attempted to initiate conversations, but I merely reacted to whatever he said without truly responding. Upon arriving at my apartment building, he pulled over and opened the door for me. Concerned, he asked if everything was alright since I hadn't uttered a word to him since we left the restaurant. I assured him that I was fine and that we would talk later. I figured out when he would likely be home, and I sent him a text to check if he had arrived safely and to express my gratitude for the amazing evening we had shared. He responded without mentioning my strange behavior as we left the restaurant.

We spent the entire week texting each other and agreed to go out again that weekend. I tried to mentally prepare myself on how to behave during and after dinner. As usual, he picked me up from my apartment and carried himself with respect, responsibility, and honor. This time, we went to a different restaurant. Throughout the meal, we chatted away, as we always had plenty to talk about. I'm not sure if he did it intentionally or if he wanted to gauge my reaction, but at one point while we were talking, he reached out his hand to hold mine. I instinctively pulled my hand away, causing him to stop talking and look at me. Realizing what I had done, I quickly pretended that I was simply scratching my arm. He smiled and resumed the conversation.

During our drive home, he asked if he could pose a personal and sensitive question. I reassured him that he could ask me anything. He emphasized that he wanted an honest answer and that he wouldn't judge me. He inquired about whether I had a boyfriend and the nature of our relationship. I explained that I had recently ended a relationship just before starting to work for Eric. I mentioned that it had been a good relationship, but something was missing, and we couldn't quite figure it out, leading to our breakup.

His next question caught me off guard. He asked if I had ever experienced sexual abuse, either as a child or an adult. I fell silent and refused to answer his question. He could see the anger and tears welling up in my eyes. Sensing my discomfort, he reassured me that it was okay if I didn't want to discuss it. After a moment of silence, he asked if I had ever considered speaking to a psychologist about it. I shook my head, thinking to myself, "I'm African, and we don't openly talk to others about our problems. We handle them ourselves." But then I questioned how well that approach had been working for me.

When we arrived at my building, he

remained in the car and made a request. He asked if, before I got out of the car, it would be alright for him to talk to his psychologist friend about me. He mentioned that she was a skilled professional, and she happened to be a lady. I was taken aback, as I had never had someone suggest such a thing to me before. I simply told him that I would think about it, unsure of how to respond.

That night, sleep eluded me as I tossed and turned in bed, consumed by thoughts of our conversation. I couldn't decide whether I should feel insulted or cared for by his words. It struck me that throughout our text and phone conversations, he had never mentioned this topic until the third day. He explained that he wanted to see if I was still pondering it or if I had reached a decision. I asked him what had led him to believe that I had been abused. He replied that the anger he saw in my eyes whenever I pulled away or recoiled from his touch had given it away. I had no idea that I carried such rage within me.

As the weekend arrived, he once again asked what I would like to do. I admitted that I would go through with it, solely because I genuinely liked him. He chuckled, stood up, and seemed about to hug me, but then hesitated and remained in place. Sensing his uncertainty, I reassured him that it was okay to hug me. A smile spread across his face, and he enveloped me in a warm, tight embrace. Without delay, he called the psychologist, and we engaged in a lengthy conversation, setting up an appointment.

And that is how I found myself here, sitting in your office today.

Psychologist

I s this the first time that you are sharing this with anyone?" the psychologist asked.

"Yes," I replied.

"So, how do you feel talking about this with a stranger?" she inquired further.

"Relieved, I have never felt so light," I admitted.

"Why have you not talked to anyone about this?" she probed.

"When I was little, I was scared. They said that they would deny it and threatened that if I tell anyone, they would harm my family members. Then, when I grew up, I was ashamed of myself because I always thought that it was my fault," I explained.

The psychologist then shifted the conversation. "I understand that you have a journal," she mentioned.

"Yes," I confirmed.

"May I take a look?" she requested.

I handed over my journal to the psychologist, who simply flipped through the pages and placed it on the side table.

"I understand that you are hurt, traumatized, and burdened by shame," she began. "But you need to let go and put these horrible experiences behind you. Allow them to remain in your past so that they will not continue to affect your present and future. I observed you telling your story. You had your journal, but you did not look at it even once, which indicates that you have been storing it all inside. Losing the journal or burning it (which is what we will do at the end of this session) will not change the fact that you were constantly abused. However, erasing it from the memory box within you might help minimize the pain and, perhaps, eventually eliminate it completely."

I started sobbing. "I thought that I had forgotten all about these experiences. After my first sexual abuse, I started having these nightmares that would not go away. I can still remember most of the nightmares."

"The first time I had one, I cried out in pain because I was subjected to a painful condition. I cannot remember what transpired between me, my sister, and the 'nice' neighbor but I know that my sister said something, and was reaping the skin off her back. She was in so much pain and was crying. I could not bear it. I was also crying and pleading with him to let her go and punish me instead."

"He refused and told me that I made him do that to my sister and that it will get worse if I ever talk about what he had done. My sister woke me up because she said that I was crying and pleading with someone. I had my hands held together the way I had it in my dream. As soon as I opened my tear-filled eyes, I grabbed my sister and hugged her. She was confused but she hugged me back and asked what had happened in my dream. I kept quiet for some time and told her that I did not remember but that it was a bad dream where both of us were severely injured."

"I thought to myself that if I told her about my dream, it is as good as telling on the neighbor and it means that my dream would become our reality. So, I refused to tell her."

The days that followed were filled with difficulty sleeping. Every time I closed my eyes, the nightmare would play out in front of me like a movie on a big screen television.

There was another nightmare that I can still recall vividly. It took place after the "nice" neighbor impregnated our nanny. At that time, I had no understanding of how someone could have a child growing inside their stomach, the science of pregnancy. When we played house, we would place a pillow or towel under our clothes to pretend we were pregnant.

I remember watching our nanny remove her clothing during her pregnancy, expecting whatever was underneath to simply fall off. To my amazement, her abdomen appeared large and rounded. I thought to myself that she must be eating too much and using the bathroom more frequently than necessary. It was only later that I realized her enlarged stomach was due to the presence of a baby, not excessive food consumption.

Then came the nightmare where the "nice" neighbor cut open the nanny's stomach and forcefully extracted the baby. Blood was everywhere, and I woke up screaming in terror.

After we left that state and went to live with my mother and other siblings, the frequency of the nightmares reduced. They were no longer a constant presence, but the memories still haunted me.

Then, afterwards, as I started building resilience, like when I stood up against the generous neighbor and yelled at the pedophile on the bus, the nightmares began to fade away to the point where I almost forgot about them. I believed that burying the whole experience deep inside and suppressing it would make it disappear. Well, it did for a while, until a few years after I broke up with my second boyfriend when the nightmares resurfaced. This time, it wasn't a younger version of myself being tortured, but an adult me. Unlike when I was younger, I tried to fight back and save my sister from punishment on my behalf. I woke up sweaty, struggling to let my sister go. I shared this dream with my niece, mentioning that the last time I had a dream like that was during my mid-teenage years. When she asked if I knew what triggered the dream, I denied having any knowledge of the factors that could have caused such a nightmare.

A few days later, I was listening to a pastor's podcast where he talked about people holding onto their past experiences. He presented it as if they had no right to hold the past against those who violated them. His words pierced through my heart like a two-edged sword, and I physically felt the pain of his words. It felt as though I had consumed something I shouldn't have, leaving me nauseated and sick to my stomach.

I reached out to my niece and discussed what the pastor had said, expressing how it felt like he was referring to me. I told her that what hurt so deeply about his words was the fact that he didn't address the victim of the abuse or acknowledge the trauma it caused in their life. He didn't discuss how the victim could heal from such trauma or suggest ways to overcome the damage caused by these abuses. Instead, he sat in his studio, passing judgment and condemning the victims who hadn't moved on from the abuse, claiming they had no right to hold the past against their abusers. I'm not saying that we should hold grudges and refuse to forgive, but in this case, I felt that he should have acknowledged the wrongs that were done before condemning the victims of these crimes. I briefly shared with my niece what happened to me as a young girl and how it affected my life. Tears welled up as I recalled all the horrible tortures I endured. I told her that I had put those experiences behind me, but for some reason, they were resurfacing. She was the first person to mention therapy to me, but I dismissed the idea of talking to anyone, especially a stranger, about this part of my history. She insisted that I needed to heal from my past and that if I didn't, it would continue to resurface, even when I thought I had forgotten about it. She said that if I didn't want to do it for myself, I should do it for the young innocent girl whose innocence was cruelly taken from her.

Holding my hands, she said to me, "It's okay to cry, just let it out. You have been through a lot. You have shown such bravery in surviving what you've experienced. That was an immense burden for an adult, let alone a child. Don't keep it bottled up any longer. Release it. Let it all out. It's a positive step that you're talking about it. It will aid in your healing process. You need to heal from your past in order to face the future. You don't want to ruin another good relationship because of what happened in the past. You have already suffered enough at the hands of these wicked men. The more you hold onto the pain of the past, the more you continue to suffer and hurt yourself, as well as the good people around you."

Aftermath

I walked out of the counseling room and into the waiting area. To my right, I saw Darren sitting in a corner, patiently waiting for me to finish my session. He had been with me the entire time, supporting me through the lengthy session that lasted the whole day. When I caught sight of him, I didn't know how to react. Tears welled up in my eyes, and I walked straight into his waiting arms. He held me tightly, allowing me to cry on his chest. He kept trying to soothe me, making it difficult for my tears to subside. He whispered reassuring words, saying, "it's okay! You're safe now! You don't need to suffer anymore! I'm here with you! No one will ever hurt you again! Take a deep breath!" It took some time for me to calm down, and once I did, I glanced at his shirt, which was stained with a combination of my makeup, tears, and snot. He didn't mind at all. All he said was, "let me take you home."

The drive back home was quiet. Darren kept checking on me, making sure I was okay. He took me to his home, which I had never been to before. As soon as we stepped off the elevator and into his living room, he told me to make myself comfortable and feel at home. He briefly showed me around, mentioning that he would prepare some food. He had ordered takeout while waiting for me to finish therapy. I offered to help him, but he declined, insisting that it was his treat. I went and sat down on his couch, patiently waiting while he got the food ready.

While we were eating, Darren began making small talk, asking me how I liked the food. Then, he mentioned that he had two questions for me and wanted me to answer honestly. My heart skipped a beat because I wasn't prepared to discuss what happened in the counseling room during my session. He noticed the change in my demeanor and reassured me that he wouldn't ask about it until I was ready to talk. Instantly, my happiness returned.

His first question caught me off guard because I wasn't expecting it. He asked if I would officially be his girlfriend. Tears welled up in my eyes, and all I could do was nod in agreement. He got up, walked over to me, held me, and asked if it was okay to ask his second question. Once again, I nodded in agreement, overwhelmed with emotions and unable to speak. He asked if I would like to stay over since it was getting late. I looked up at him, let out a mix of laughter and tears, and silently said yes. He was overjoyed, kissed me on the forehead, and returned to his seat.

After dinner, he explained that he wanted us to take things slowly, considering what I had been through. He gave me the option of either sleeping in his room or in the guest bedroom. I smiled at him and told him I would be in his room with him. It was an unfamiliar place, and I didn't want to be alone. He showed me the shower and provided everything I might need for the night. By the time I finished showering, he had already cleaned up the dishes and was ready to take his own shower. I lay at the edge of the bed, almost on the verge of falling off. He smiled at me, laid next to me, and asked if it was okay to hold me. I drifted off to sleep peacefully, feeling safe and secure in his arms, like a baby.

A Note From The Author

Thank you so much for reading this book. Everything in this story, up until the therapy session and meeting Darren, is based on true events from my own life. My journey hasn't been easy, and I am still in the process of healing from the trauma I experienced from the age of six into my young adulthood. Living in fear and shame is not a life anyone would choose. Writing this book is a part of my healing process.

The main purpose of this book is to give a voice to the voiceless. My voice was taken away from me, and this book represents me reclaiming it. I no longer live in fear or shame; I am now bold and brave. My hope is that people all over the world, especially women who have experienced or are currently experiencing similar trauma, will find healing through this book and feel empowered to talk about their own experiences in order to heal.

I want all of you to know that:
You are BOLD!
You are BRAVE!
You are not defined by fear!
You are not alone in your fearlessness!

Printed in the USA
CPSIA information can be obtained
at www.ICGtesting.com
LVHW052325161023
761015LV00025BA/206/J